Parson's Porch Books

www.parsonsporchbooks.com

A Better Ewe

ISBN: 978-1-951472-52-8

Copyright © 2020 by Beth Murdock Hess

Inspired by the New Teacher Academy
At
River Ridge High School
Senior Class 2020

Photo Credit:
Mike Carlson Photography
Moments by Michelle and Beth Hess

Edited by:
Kathryn Cole, Amanda Salas, Faith Sanchez, Tori Senior
and my loving husband, Rick Hess

A Special Thank You to:
Leanne John, Agricultural Science teacher at
Zephyrhills High School

Dedicated to my precious grandchildren,
Connor and Avery

Introduction

As a child, I spent time visiting my grandparents' farm. Life on a farm builds character throughout life. I remember the simple lessons of my grandparents: Faith that it would rain, Hope that the seeds germinate, and Love during dinnertime where everyone gathered for a family meal. I always imagined their farm animals as characters acting out their roles. I cherish that time, and even though the setting of *A Better Ewe* is more tropical, I hope anyone can discover purpose by reading this book.

I also hope my own grandchildren will be inspired by this story, just as I was by the visits to my grandparents' farm.

Beth Murdock Hess

A Better Ewe

"Welcome to the farm! We are all here to support you. There are many different animals here, but you seem special. Are you a sheep?" The farmer adjusted her hat as she welcomed her new friend.

"I'm not a sheep; I'm a EWE, pronounced like 'you,' which is a *special* name for a sheep. I like to stay by myself and not mix with the other animals."

"You seem like you are having a hard time adjusting to your new life here. Being isolated with a new group can be hard, but I can help you adjust. I can help you become a better EWE! I like your confidence, but you can learn a lot by making friends with the other animals. Here on the farm, we know we need each other, even though we are different. Don't ever forget that because it may save your life one day."

Lesson #1:

Be confident while remaining open to other views

The next morning, Ewe got up extra early to take a stroll around the farm. She did not want to mingle, so she decided to sneak out of the pen and venture out to the field. The sun was just rising, and she was excited to see her new home. She ate grass and moved closer to the fence, far from the safety of the farm. There was a sign she wanted to read in the distance, but she was too far away to see it.

As she neared the fence, she sounded out the words: No "Trè" "spas" "sing." She read the words again and decided this must be French. She remembered her birth farm, with the beautiful white trellis with flowers growing in and out of the slats, and she knew this must be a wonderful place to visit. A "Trè" "Spas" "Sing" must be a spa with a flower trellis and singing, yes...lots of singing. "That sounds like a wonderful place," she thought, and she whispered, "I am going to go there."

Lesson #2:

Do not assume you already know everything you'll need to know in your lifetime

When Ewe got back, she was so excited about her new discovery, but she was *not* excited when she realized that she had missed breakfast. She butted the door of the farm house, stepping right over the dog, to ask for a special breakfast. The farmer's son opened the door. He was dressed to start his chores on the farm; he was not excited to see a sheep at his door.

The Ewe decided to make up a story instead of telling him the truth. She slyly stated, "I was kept up late by the cows last night, and I overslept this morning. May I have some breakfast, please" ...and with a grin, she added, "maybe some French toast would be nice," as she remembered her new French words, *Trè spas sing*.

Lesson #3:

Always tell the truth

The farmer's son was not amused that this sheep thought she could do what she wanted. He knew he had to feed her, but he was not making French toast for a sheep. Instead he led her back to the pen and refilled the trough, which brought an abundance of other animals back to snack with her. Since they were all eating, no animals tried to make friends, which was *fine* with her.

Nevertheless, that night the cows were left in the field, causing quite a ruckus of mooing, which really did keep her awake. All night she kept the chickens and the goats up by complaining about the noise. It never dawned on her that she was as much of a problem to them as the mooing cows were to her.

Lesson #4:

Don't complain; instead, devote your energy
to your purpose

15

She had spent two days on the farm, and she decided her new *Secret Spa* was surely a better place for her. After all, she was extra special because she was a Ewe.

The farm had so many rules: Stay in the pen, eat breakfast early, and get along with all of the animals. She didn't see why she needed to do any of these because these rules did not apply to her. So, she knocked over the feed sack left by the farmer's son, and she left the pen to go visit the French "Trè spas."

Lesson #5:

Even if you don't like the rules,
they are there for a reason

When the animals woke up, the cows were coming in, knocking over the barrels for their milk, and the roosters were pecking at each other, grumbling that the feed on the ground was only for them. The goats butted heads because they had gotten no sleep, and the tranquil farm had become a place of disarray. They looked at each other, questioning, "What has happened to our farm?"

One brave Bull looked around and said, "We are all here except for the new Ewe. Since the Ewe arrived, we have all been in trouble." The farm dog stated, "Let's find the Ewe who caused this chaos," but the wise Bull said, "These are hard times for all of us; maybe she needs compassionate friends instead of a farm full of enemies."

Lesson #6:

Be a rebuilder, even when you grow weary

The animals knew Bull was right. The tired cows mooed in agreement, the chickens decided to share the feed, and the goats realized ramming their heads only gave them headaches; it did not focus on solving the problem. It was the dog who finally said he would go look for her. He ate his breakfast and set out to find her.

After an hour of running in the fields, he saw the Ewe in the distance, but there was a problem. She was not in the fence! No animal had ever ventured beyond the fence, and this was a serious issue. She was heading to the new field, but by doing this, he knew she was trespassing, and she was getting close to the dangerous area they had only heard about. Trespassing was forbidden on the farm. That was the first rule all animals learned, but there she was.

Dog ran quickly, but the more he barked, the faster she moved. "Why did she not heed the warning? No Trespassing," he thought, as he ran back to the farm to get help.

Lesson #7:

Never give up when you can help out

All farm animals knew that it was easier to get beyond the fence than it was to get back. One time Bull told a story of something called Barbed Wire, a prickly wire that lined the edge of the fence that cut the skin if it ever pricked an animal. Most frightened animals would try to retreat when they realized they were beyond the fence, but they would get cut deeply as they frantically tried to navigate the barbed wire, attempting to rectify the mistake they had made.

Animals who ventured out usually became very sick from their wounds, and sometimes they had to ride in the wagon that never seemed to bring them back.

Bull said that the animals had to help Ewe, even if she had broken all the rules and had lied about the cows. The animals neighed, clucked, and rammed their heads, but finally all agreed to help. Even the cows, who were the last to join in, realized that helping was the only choice.

Lesson #8:

Some things in life are worth
overcoming your doubts and fears

As the animals planned their rescue, Ewe continued her adventure. "Those silly farm animals are so narrow-minded," she thought, "They probably don't even know French words, and they have no spirit of adventure," adding arrogantly, "I am so glad I am not like them."

She had found a beautiful path covered in trees leading to the "Trè Spas," which seemed to consume her French dreams. She did not even notice that it was becoming late in the afternoon. All she could focus on were her own desires.

Lesson #9:

Know your life plan and focus on that

As she topped the ridge that had been blocking her view, she expected to see a beautiful white trellis and a welcoming barn where she could stay the night and receive her spa treatment. Instead, she saw a very dark overgrown grouping of trees. The lovely green path had been slowly transformed into gnarled tripping roots poking up and suffocating Spanish moss hanging down. For the first time, she was afraid, and the screeching from the vultures and the rustling from the forest magnified her fright, making her regret her decision. When she turned around, eyes were hidden in the woods, and she recognized that she was lost.

Lesson #10:

Even in dark times, there are
valuable lessons to be learned

She wished she had listened to the farmer who had told her all the animals helped each other. She wished she had befriended the ones who were so different from her. Instead, she had focused on her own desires, rather than embracing their differences. She remembered the cows and how she had lied about them. She thought of the chickens and recalled knocking over their feed, and she regretted judging the goats ramming their heads together, thinking how stupid they must be.

As she sat on the roots and twigs, she started to cry. She even remembered the dog who was barking in the field. Instead of turning to him, she ran away, thinking he would spoil her adventure. She found herself missing that dog, making her even sadder.

Lesson #11:

Listening and reflecting on what others say offers direction

29

For the first time in her life, she recognized that she needed others. Before, others had just been a way to get to where she wanted to go, but now, she saw them as a lifeline.

What was that called? She thought for a long time, and then it hit her. She needed companionship. The Ewe had never realized that she needed a friend because she only cared about herself.

As she closed her eyes to rest, she wasn't thinking of the field. She wasn't imagining a day of pampering at the "Trè Spas Sing." She was remembering how important safety felt. She was imagining having dinner with her friends, and she thought of the dog. At first, she had thought he was lazy, but now she saw him as a faithful companion.

Lesson #12:

Companionship and community diminish
the feelings of loneliness

She suddenly awoke to a frightening sound. She couldn't identify it, but she knew it was getting closer. It sounded sneaky. It would move and then stop. She was unsure which direction to go, so she didn't move, but it did. She couldn't see but she knew she had to move away from the sound. Something was different now as she moved blindly along the path. Her fleece was damp, and her hooves were embedded in mud which made it harder for her to move.

The ground was no longer solid; she was in the swamp. She had heard an animal once talk about the swamp, but it sounded so dirty, so she didn't listen.

They had tried to warn her of the dangers out there, but she didn't care because it didn't seem to affect her. She always thought she knew more than the others.

She wished that she had listened. Just once.

Lesson #13:

Wisdom is heard clearly through listening

Back at the farm, the animals made their plan. The cows would get out of the pen and scatter to distract the farmer and her son. The chickens would peck the goats to cause quite a disruption, and mules would knock over the feed and spill the water in the trough. While this was going on, Dog, Bull, and the mares would sneak away to find the sheep. They knew they could travel faster than many of the other animals on the farm and could use their strength to rescue Ewe.

They did not know how she would react, but they knew they had to try to reach her because she was in danger.

Lesson #14:

Making plans and working collaboratively
is the path to success

The animals refused to give up even though Ewe had been so mean. The animals knew their job was to teach Ewe to trust them first, and then convince her to return with them so she could reach her full potential on the farm. She had been so stubborn; Ewe had been very distant and had not even tried, but none of that seemed to matter now. They had a job to do. Even though they had not been trained for this task, the animals knew they must respond and trust their instincts.

They followed the beam of moonlight moving quickly across the field. All of the animals had been inspired to act from lessons they had learned on the farm. Bull had strength because he had pulled a plow to till the field many times. The mares had power from years of leading the carriage in the town's parade. Dog had perseverance, being the loyal overseer and the most trusted animal on the farm. Each was inspired to move quickly and powerfully for the sake of Ewe.

As they ran, it was Dog who led the chant, "Rescue Ewe! Rescue Ewe! Rescue Ewe!"

Lesson #15:

There is always someone out there
who cares enough to act

Ewe was wet and stuck. The silence of the black night was only interrupted by a sound she had never heard before. It was so faint, almost inaudible, yet there was a rippling sound moving closer to her through the water, coupled with another sound from the far distance - one she definitely could not distinguish.

It was like the cadence of a chant, interrupted by something ominous breaking the water.

She strained to remember anything that could help her fight back, and she recalled the animals on the farm. The goats butted heads in a playful battle. The mares stomped their hooves to protect their foals from an approaching coyote, and the dog barked ferociously to turn away a fox who was threatening the hens.

Both sounds inched forward, one that was frightening; one that was comforting. She strained to hear what comforted her.

Lesson #16:

When you are stuck, don't give up!

The rescue team had reached the fence. None had ever trespassed before, but they knew this was important. The mares and Dog were able to leap over, but Bull had to charge through. He closed his eyes and bolted forward, ripping the barbed wire as it clawed into his hide. The wire had to be torn down or Ewe could not return. Bull made the sacrifice of his own skin, plowing through the wire for her.

All the animals were now outside of the fence, and they moved as a force down the path leading to their destination.

Their paws and hooves became damp as they approached the swamp.

Just as they neared the transition of mud to water, they saw Ewe. She was faint in the distance, hidden by the undergrowth surrounding the swamp, but they had found her.

Lesson #17:

The greatest sacrifice one can make
is the sacrifice for a friend

They were not the only creatures who had found her. They spied a massive alligator within yards of Ewe, one who thrived on those who innocently ventured into the swampy wilderness. The gator was creeping up, and Ewe could not move.

It was Dog that made the first move. Without giving a second thought or discussing his plan, he ran as a greyhound would, lunging forward right in front of the gator, now only a few feet from its next victim. He swam between the gator and Ewe, knowing it would choose the closer of the two and follow its new prey for a midnight meal.

The mares and Bull pulled Ewe from the mud and got her to safety. She could not even respond because everything happened so quickly. They surrounded her and led her back, following the trail left by the droplets of blood, sacrificed by Bull. They reached the fence, crossing back into the safety of the pasture.

They led Ewe home, passing by the sign now on the ground that read, "No Trespassing." Ewe finally understood the real meaning of these words.

Lesson #18:

Obstacles in life present opportunities for growth

The rescue crew and Ewe arrived as the sun was rising. It was a glorious morning. The farmer's son had left early to tend to the cows and repair the fence. The animals all gathered to welcome their companion home and to care for Bull. No one questioned why Ewe left; they only offered encouragement that she had returned.

It was Ewe who spoke up first. Ewe raised her head away from the feed, although she was very hungry, and thanked her friends for their forgiveness and unconditional love. Ewe asked all the animals to gather so she could share what she had learned.

Lesson #19:

Character is developed through
life lessons learned

When all around her could hear, Ewe started to speak, "I have learned so much about life in such a short time, and I want to thank you as I share. You are each so important to me, and it took this experience for me to recognize some things in life that I have taken for granted. These are the lessons I hope you will remember when you face struggles in life."

1. Be confident while remaining open to other views
2. Do not assume you already know everything you'll need
   to know in your lifetime
3. Always tell the truth
4. Don't complain; instead, devote your energy to your
   purpose
5. Even if you don't like the rules, they are there for a
   reason
6. Be a rebuilder, even when you grow weary
7. Never give up when you can help out
8. Some things in life are worth overcoming your doubts
   and fears
9. Know your life plan and focus on that
10. Even in dark times, there are valuable lessons to be
    learned

11. Listening and reflecting on what others say offers direction
12. Companionship and community diminish the feelings of loneliness
13. Wisdom is heard clearly through listening
14. Making plans and working collaboratively is the path to success
15. There is always someone out there who cares enough to act
16. When you are stuck, don't give up
17. The greatest sacrifice one can make is the sacrifice for a friend
18. Obstacles in life present opportunities for growth
19. Character is developed through life lessons learned

And with that, Ewe started looking around. She was proud of sharing the lessons she had learned, but as she glanced at her friends, a tear ran down her cheek. She looked into the faces of each of them, taking time with her eyes to say thank you for what they had done, but then she cleared her throat, and from her heart, spoke the words, "Where is Dog?"

The mares neighed as they realized Dog had not returned with them. Bull, covered in bandages, looked around the barnyard.

The triumphant celebration and beautiful shared lessons surrendered to a solemn atmosphere of realization.

Dog had not returned.

The frozen somber moment was interrupted as the farmer's son arrived in "the wagon." Ewe remembered hearing that animals that became very sick had to ride in the wagon that never seemed to bring them back.

She started to cry even more as she feared her friend would be picked up from the steps of the farmhouse, carried off to never be seen again.

All the animals were silent as the farmer's son got out of the seat and walked to the back, lowering the gate of the wagon.

But this time was different. He wasn't putting something in the wagon.

He was taking something out.

He had rescued Dog, who had survived the attack of the alligator.

As he carried the dog in his arms by the animals, Dog lifted his head and faintly whispered, "Never give up hope. It is the best lesson of all to become *A Better Ewe*."

Ewe knew this was the final lesson for her to learn.

The farmer's son did not stop at the steps this time where the farm dog usually slept beside the white trellis, but instead, he carried the dog inside the house, humming a gentle song to comfort him.

They knew that no matter what, they could always count on each other, and by having friends to count on, they knew she would always be *A Better Ewe*.

CPSIA information can be obtained
at www.ICGtesting.com
Printed in the USA
LVHW061402170720
660979LV00002B/2

9 781951 472528